Wheels Around Caithness and Sutherland

by
Robert Grieves

A well-known garage business in Caithness is that owned by J. & G. Sutherland of Halkirk, founded in 1918 and one of the oldest established Rover dealerships in the UK. Sutherlands moved to the wooden premises pictured here in Crescent Street, Halkirk in 1946 which had been a former joiner's shop. Today's garage was built in 1959 on the same site. This scene from 1950 shows the old garage with JS 7582, a 1947 Riley 1.5 litre saloon being checked over. Familiar forecourt signs advertise Dunlop tyres, Esso petrol, KLG spark plugs and Wakefield Castrol oil. Present owner and motor enthusiast Edward Sutherland is well-known for his collection of splendidly restored vintage cars.

ISBN 1 84033 201 8

Bonar Bridge spans the channel connecting the inner Dornoch Firth with the Kyle of Sutherland. This 1954 scene looking towards Bonar Bridge village depicts the crossing of 1893 which replaced Thomas Telford's original 1812 bridge, destroyed by a flood in 1892. In turn this bridge was superseded by today's graceful structure in 1973. Driving towards the camera is MAD 597, an Austin A70 Hereford registered in Gloucestershire in 1952 and probably owned by visiting holidaymakers on tour.

INTRODUCTION

Caithness and Sutherland, Scotland's northernmost mainland counties, were regarded at one time as almost isolated outposts by those who knew no better. These counties nevertheless enjoyed both rail and road transport communications no later than many of the more populous southern areas, and in fact one of the earliest 'cars' in Britain was a steam-powered three-wheeler built for the Earl of Caithness as early as 1860. Along with his wife and the Revd William Ross of Kintore, Aberdeenshire, the Earl and his steam car successfully managed the 145 miles from Inverness to his castle at Barrogill, the late Queen Mother's Scottish residence and renamed Castle of Mey. The appalling condition of the road north o'er the Ord at that time can only be imagined, but even the dreaded climbs at Helmsdale and Berriedale presented no difficulty to the steamer, which had been built by one Thomas Rickett of Buckingham, who was also present on the journey, acting as stoker during the trip. Lady Caithness is reputed to have declared on this occasion that if Caithness (her husband) blew up then she was quite ready to accompany him. Unfortunately for road vehicles, legislation soon followed which cut legal speeds to a ridiculously low limit and effectively stopped their development until the final years of the nineteenth century.

During the very last years of Queen Victoria's reign and the first few of King Edward VII's, when motor cars were in their infancy, it was only the very wealthy who could afford what were to them often little more than expensive toys. The motor registration mark for the county of Sutherland was NS, introduced in January 1904; Frederick Sutherland Leveson Gower of Morvich Lodge, Rogart, nephew of the 3rd Duke of Sutherland, was issued with NS 1 for his dark green 12 h.p. Napier tonneau (the Duke himself had owned no less than three 12 h.p. Panhards prior to the requirement for motor licensing). Andrew Carnegie, the American industrialist who had emigrated from Dunfermline and ultimately became the world's richest man, had his Sutherland home at Skibo Castle and owned a number of NS registered motor vehicles. These included not only cars but a battery-powered bus NS 15 in 1904 which was appropriately green and presumably used for the conveyance of guests and also a yellow Argyll lorry (NS 79) in 1907.

The twentieth century saw all sorts of attempts – some definitely downright different and verging on the eccentric – to travel between Scotland's north-eastern extremity at John O' Groats and England's south-western equivalent at Land's End, some wheeled examples of which are illustrated in the following pages.

That gruelling test of man and motor car, the Monte Carlo Rally, first started from John O' Groats in 1926. In that year the Hon. Victor Bruce, driving an AC, won the event. The following year, also in an AC, his wife Mary Petre (better known as The Hon. Mrs Victor Bruce) also started from John O' Groats and won the Ladies' Cup, having driven single-handed all the way to Monte Carlo. Another well-known lady competitor was Amy Johnson in 1936.

Sutherland, despite being one of Scotland's largest counties, is sparsely populated and accordingly its registration numbers climbed slowly over the years. By June 1964 they had only reached NS 5683 when they were replaced by the three letter index mark with number then letter suffix, which in Sutherland commenced ANS _ _ _ B, as a A was not used.

Caithness numbers rose somewhat faster and reached the SK 9999 limit in August 1963 when they moved on to an ASK series with no suffix, until August 1964 when the ASK _ _ _ B suffix series started. Incidentally, away back in 1904 when the Caithness numbers were introduced, SK 1 was issued to Col. Edward William Horne of Stirkoke, Wick, for his 11 h.p. Clement.

As usual in this family of 'Wheels' books, my goal is simply to include a variety of illustrations of wheeled vehicles native to the area. I hope the following selection will perhaps kindle a few memories and possibly encourage younger readers to find out more about a subject often neglected by social historians. Some of the illustrations have come from the Johnston Collection held by the Wick Historical Society, for whose permission to publish I gratefully acknowledge Iain Sutherland. Others whose help I must record include John Aldridge, London; Alan Brotchie, Aberdour; John Gillham, London; Angus Mackenzie, Scourie; William Grant, Keiss; Neil Harrold, Wick; Phyllis Campbell, Wick; Willie Munro, Lairg; Willie Milne, Inverness; Ian Maclean, Bishopton; W.A.C. Smith, Glasgow; Gordon Steele, Inverness; Edward Sutherland, Halkirk; and the late Gordon Burr, Tongue.

Situated at the most north-easterly point of mainland Scotland, John O' Groats has provided sufficient reason over the years for countless folks to drive, walk, run, cycle, roller-skate or whatever all the way to or from the opposite corner of the country – Land's End in Cornwall. The two places are 876 miles apart, the greatest distance between any two points on the British mainland. One of the more unusual end-to-end marathons was made by this elderly gentleman in 1904 when he pushed a barrow all the way between the two extremities. Visible inside it is an old greatcoat and a pair of boots, while painted on the handles is '2,000 miles walk' suggesting that a double journey and more was intended. Embroidered on his cap and painted on the side of the barrow is 'R. Carlisle' which was his name. Robert Carlisle was a Scot who lived in Cornwall but was a native of Edinburgh. Incredibly, he had previously made the same marathon journey in

1879 with his wheelbarrow and was to do it yet again in 1906! An entry during 1879 in one of the John O' Groats Hotel visitors' books reads: 'I Robert Carlisle late of Edinburgh and St Austell Cornwall on a 2,000 mile tour with a wheelbarrow started from Land's End on Tuesday September 23 and arrived here on Tuesday 21 October after a tough passage of 25 days as I did not travel Sundays. Left John O' Groats Hotel at 12 noon on Wednesday October 22 for Land's End via Inverness, Aberdeen, Dundee, Edinburgh, Berwick, Durham, York, Sheffield, Leeds, Bradford, Manchester, Lincoln, Cambridge, London, Brighton and Exeter. My speculation is to show it is possible for a Scotsman to do a feat of endurance.' Later visitors' books for 1904 and 1906 again show entries for Robert, who I suspect was perhaps a shade eccentric. This scene was captured by Alexander Johnston outside his photographer's studio in Wick Market Place as the strange sight passed through the town, with an attendant group of somewhat incredulous youngsters.

The picture on the front cover illustrates the start of the successful 1900 John O' Groats to Land's End journey made by Hubert Egerton of Norwich in a Locomobile. Early in 1903 his brother Justin Reginald Egerton set out on a similar attempt. Our photo shows a light covering of snow at the commencement of his January journey at a windy John O' Groats, with Reginald Egerton (as he was usually known) seen shaking hands and holding on to his hat at the same time. The car was a somewhat obscure make imported from Germany called the Primus, built by a company which also produced sewing machines and bicycles (Primus cars only had a short existence, being built between 1899 and 1903). The one pictured was a 7 h.p. model with belt drive. Egerton had a vested interest in the success of this journey since his Ipswich business partnership of Botwood & Egerton, motor engineers and coachbuilders, were agents for the Primus car. However, because of many troubles, caused by a combination of bad weather and mechanical problems – and even catching fire – it was decided to abandon the attempt to reach Land's End and settle for a safe return home to Ipswich in Suffolk instead, which was achieved. From the photograph it would appear that half of the local population in Groats had turned out to wish Egerton luck on his journey! Note also the huge extra petrol tank fitted temporarily behind the bulkhead which contained 30 gallons but must have somewhat restricted legroom within the car. **5**

The first end-to-end motor run to be completed by a woman was made in September 1903, and this journey's end scene at John O' Groats Hotel was taken shortly after the arrival of the party from Land's End. The feat was particularly remarkable considering the driver was a nineteen year old girl (from Kilkenny, Ireland) who had her first driving lessons shortly before the successful 900 mile journey. Miss Murison's family originally came from Orkney and were friendly with George Johnston, co-founder and managing director of the Paisley-based Mo-Car Syndicate which built the Arrol–Johnston car driven by her (we do not know her first name as the contemporary newspaper reports only refer to her as 'Miss Murison'). Johnston obviously realised the publicity potential of such a journey made by a member of the fair sex in days when male domination still ruled the infant world of the automobile. That one of his cars should successfully complete what was then something of a marathon, and especially when driven by a young lady with no technical skills whatsoever, was valuable advertising material. To modern eyes the Arrol–Johnston car seems a strange beast, appearing more like a carriage awaiting a couple of horses to be hitched on. Passengers in the rear seats faced backwards, while the amazing driving position was *behind* the first row of seats which would certainly not comply with today's regulations. Indeed even a century ago the design of this car was outmoded, although its reliability was such that it remained in production in this form until 1905.

This is typical of the horse-drawn coaches operated in Victorian and Edwardian days by the Sutherland Arms Hotel, Lairg, when passengers, mails and goods were carried by this means from the railhead at Lairg on separate services to Lochinver, Scourie and Tongue. The business was founded by Gray & Murray in 1878 and stables were established en route at Altnaharra, midway to Tongue, and at Overscaig and Achfarry on the Scourie route. In 1905 the first motor vehicle arrived and in 1906 the business was sold to Wm. Wallace of Oban, who disposed of the remaining horses and coaches and introduced a fleet of Albion wagonettes to improve and expand the mail services, adopting the name of Sutherland Motor Traffic Company. A contemporary report quoted Mr Wallace as stating that any one of his Albions could do in ten hours what it used to take three or four pairs of horses two days to accomplish. In 1920 the company was registered with the title Sutherland Transport & Trading Co. Ltd. and the automobile spares and servicing side of the business was developed, along with car hire. This view outside the hotel about 1902 shows, alongside the driver, a uniformed employee with 'Sutherland Arms Hotel' embroidered on his cap.

A steam wagon arrives at Wick railway station in the early Edwardian period pulling primitive trailers which appear to contain the contents of a family flitting. No doubt someone's treasured possessions bound for a distant destination by the Highland Railway. The advert on the station building for Maple & Co.'s 'First Class Furniture', with branches in London, Buenos Aires and Paris, is perhaps somewhat incongruous in comparison to the less than first class tables, chairs and bedsteads contained in the wagons. Whoever the unknown owners may have been, I hope they found success in their new life.

Children of today miss out on many things formerly enjoyed by older generations, but probably don't realise their loss. Simple pleasures like running alongside a steamroller for instance. 'What's a steamroller?' would probably be the child's reaction. Well, the vehicle illustrated above was typical of such a beast, this one owned by Caithness County Council and used most often on road maintenance work. After all, this was the Edwardian age and many of our roads were not paved with asphalt but merely crushed stones rolled tightly together by the type of machine pictured. This example was built by Aveling & Porter of Rochester, Kent in the early 1900s (readily identifiable by their prancing horse motif), but sadly the names of the council workmen beside their wagon somewhere near Huna are unknown.

In the years prior to World War I, the proprietrix of John O' Groats Hotel was Mrs Isabella Calder. Here we see her at the wheel of SK 150, her green Argyll 15 h.p. landaulette which was new in 1912 and was used both for the conveyance of hotel guests and local hiring. The names of the males (and dog) in attendance are not known. The Argyll was built in a palatial factory in Alexandria, Dunbartonshire which still exists today as Loch Lomond Factory Outlets, a retail clothing store but also housing, appropriately, a motor museum.

Inset is SK 340, one of three solid-tyred Wolverhampton-built Star buses operated by Robertson in the early 1920s. Apparently they were often guilty of breaking axle casings on the bumpy roads and in this view there may have been other mechanical problems, judging by the concerned faces around the open bonnet.

Col. Josiah James Robertson, trading as Alexander Robertson & Son, Bridge Street Garage, Wick, owned SK 241, an imported American Hupmobile built by the Hupp Motor Car Corporation of Detroit, Michigan and seen here at John O' Groats. This particular car was a 15/18 h.p. 6-seat tourer new in 1914 and painted black. Its electric lighting is noteworthy as this was still a relatively uncommon motoring feature at that time. Robertson was a motor agent, car hirer and dealer who also ran a general furnishing and ironmongers store in Wick. In addition, he held the Royal Mail contract in the 1920s to operate the mail bus service between Wick, Dunbeath and Helmsdale, linking the various coastal villages not served by the railway. In 1932 the bus services were acquired by the Highland Transport Co. of Inverness along with his fleet of 14-seat Chevrolets, an AJS and an Albion.

The Albion was one of the most popular chassis for commercial vehicle owners in Scotland's northern counties in the early days of transport. Robert Garden, a general merchant based in Tongue, owned NS 42 (new in 1905) and NS 17 (of 1904), both examples of the 16 h.p. A3 model and seen here leaving 'Dunvarrich', Tongue. (This was Garden's home and later the home of Peter Burr and family who came from Aberdeenshire to work for Garden and subsequently took over the business – see page 47.) Not only were these Albions used for transporting and delivering goods, but they could also be fitted with up to ten seats for passengers and their luggage. In fact, after the days of the horse-drawn stagecoaches, they were the first motors to meet the trains at Lairg station, 40 miles from Tongue, conveying well-to-do guests to various shooting lodges in the county. One such regular customer in those far-off days was Joseph Baxendale of Ben Klebrick Lodge, who later perhaps inevitably purchased his own motorised conveyance, in the shape of a 20 h.p. Crossley car in 1913.

SK 73 is a similar Albion 16 h.p. wagonette to those seen opposite, but a later model, which was delivered in February 1909 to the Caithness & Sutherland Motor Car Co. Ltd. of Olrig Street, Thurso. This pioneering concern operated the first motor mail and passenger service from Thurso to Castletown, Mey and John O' Groats and a separate service between John O' Groats and Wick. The initial shareholders when the company was formed in 1907 were Robert Garden, merchant, of Tongue; Andrew Swanson, contractor; George Anderson, accountant; William Anderson, farmer; Richard Lindsay, ironmonger; and Peter Keith and David Murray, solicitors – all of Thurso. Its immaculate appearance, apart from the mud spatters of the winter roads, suggests that this was possibly the inaugural run of SK 73. The crowd of interested Wickers outside R. S. Waters' shop (agent for the Caithness & Sutherland Motor Co.) in a now much altered part of the west end of Wick High Street, would perhaps confirm this. The well-dressed passengers underline that to travel by public transport was not cheap in those early days and the cash bag around the driver's shoulder indicates that he also collected the fares. Note also that someone has a bicycle on board to continue their journey independently.

SK 183 was a chain-driven solid-tyred 25 h.p. bus delivered in November 1912 to R. S. Waters of High Street, Wick. Bodywork on the bus incorporated a compartment for mail and panels at the rear and was built by Malcolm Bros. of Whitechapel, Wick, who had previously specialised in constructing horse-drawn carts and coaches. It was used on the Royal Mail contract between Wick and John O' Groats, formerly worked by the Caithness & Sutherland Motor Car Co. Ltd. Waters had been the company's Wick agent, based in his Wick ironmongery store, which can be glimpsed in the previous picture. This photograph shows the Halley (which was painted blue) with a local postman and its regular driver Daniel Mowatt, who became almost a local legend and remained driving buses until he retired. Despite the fact that he drove Waters' John O' Groats mail service, to the local folk it was always known as 'Denniel's Bus' (see also facing page). His son William was also a bus driver for Waters and later operated his own bus before selling out to Highland Omnibuses in 1952. The original timetable allowed two hours for the John O' Groats to Wick journey, leaving each morning at 10 a.m. and returning, to quote the contemporary advertising '35 mins after the arrival of the 3.50 train'. To this day there is a 10 a.m. journey from John **14** O' Groats to Wick, although the running time is naturally much less.

The Royal Mail and passenger bus from Thurso to John O' Groats poses around 1911 with some of the locals outside what at that time was Donald Murray's Castletown post office, ironmongery and general store (now the St Clair Arms Hotel). The bus was a Halley, built in Yoker, Glasgow and owned by the Caithness & Sutherland Motor Car Co. Ltd. Note the initials GR on the side panels of the bus, signifying that it was operating an official mail contract in the reign of King George V, who had recently gained the throne after the death of Edward VII in 1910. The driver, with his foot on the step, is thought to be George Sinclair of Mey; the local postman is second from the left.

Royal Mail at Castletown.

SK 1952 was a 16-seater Ford belonging to Robert Simon Waters of Wick, who traded as the John O' Groats Motor Co. It was bought in 1934 for his Wick to John O' Groats mail service and known as Denniel's Bus after its regular driver Daniel Mowatt. Going back to late Victorian times, the company had operated the horse-drawn Barrogill passenger coach and advertisements in the *John O' Groat Journal* for 1897 showed the departure from Huna to Wick at 7.40 a.m., returning at 4 p.m. with an extension to and from Mey on certain days.

James Begg of Four Winds Farm, Port Dunbar, was an enterprising fish merchant, cooper and haulage contractor who also operated various forms of transport in Wick, including lorries, buses and taxis. This scene at Sinclair's Central Garage in Union Street (now an extension of Mackay's Hotel) shows SK 1500, one of Begg's 'Express Motor Bus Company' 14-seaters, brand new in 1928. It was a Manchester, a rather uncommon make (note the advert on the driver's door) which was built by the Willys Overland Crossley Co. in Stockport. The bodywork was constructed in Wick by local joiner Alex (Sandy) Dunnet who was employed by Miller's Joinery but who also drove on a part-time basis for Begg and may be seen in the driving seat in this view. James Begg, wearing the soft hat, is at the garage door alongside James Y. Sinclair, the garage proprietor. The 'Express' service ran from Wick to Thurso and Wick to Dunbeath in opposition to Alex Robertson of Wick, but only operated for a few years as Begg sold his bus interests to Highland Transport in 1933 to concentrate on the haulage side of the business.

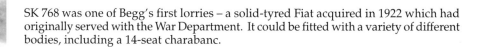

SK 768 was one of Begg's first lorries – a solid-tyred Fiat acquired in 1922 which had originally served with the War Department. It could be fitted with a variety of different bodies, including a 14-seat charabanc.

SK 1043 was a solid-tyred Leyland new in 1925, seen here in Wick with owner James Begg standing proudly at the cab door. It was used mainly for fish transport.

SX (not SK!) 2848 was a Bean which had started life in 1929 as a 14-seat bus in West Lothian and was bought by James Begg for his Wick to Dunbeath bus service. When Begg sold the buses in 1933 to concentrate on his haulage business, this one was converted to a lorry, as seen here alongside herring barrels at Wick Harbour.

In 1933 James Begg sold his bus interests to the Highland Transport Co. and in the same year purchased this new Commer lorry.

RG 8902 was an Aberdeen registered 1938 Buick owned by James Begg and used for taxi and car hire purposes.

For many years John O' Groats House Hotel has served as the local bus terminus, and this quiet scene from the late 1950s (in contrast to that seen opposite) shows two vehicles owned by Highland Omnibuses, a Guy Arab service bus on the left and a Bedford coach to the right. Neither of these is quite what it seems, however. The Guy started life during the 1939–1945 war as a utility double decker in the London Transport fleet and was purchased with many others by Scottish Omnibuses Ltd. of Edinburgh in the early 1950s. Some, such as the example seen here, had their old bodies removed and were rebodied by SOL as single deckers. They also received new registration numbers, in this case LSC 98 (K 97), which was one of eighteen similar Guy rebuilds in the Highland fleet. The Bedford was AST 829 (C5) which originated during the war as a 1942 OWB model with 29-seat austerity SMT bodywork. In 1953 the chassis was converted to forward control and it received a new 24-seat coach body by Burlingham of Blackpool to the style known as 'Baby Seagull'. By this means, both vehicles had their natural lifespan extended by several years.

The small touring coach of Highland Omnibuses in the centre of this busy 1960s view is an Alexander-bodied Albion Nimbus which was one of six (KST 50-55 / A1-6) delivered in 1956. Among the many makes of car visible are Austin, Ford, Riley, Standard, Vauxhall and with the gift of good eyesight several others. Although John O' Groats is located near the north-east tip of Scotland at Duncansby Head, Scotland's northernmost point is actually Dunnet Head, a few miles west of Groats. At the time of writing John O' Groats Hotel (octagonal like the famous Dutchman's original house) awaits refurbishment, but has been a familiar background to many photographs since it started life in Victorian times. Extensions (not particularly sympathetic ones) have been added over the years.

Since almost the dawn of the motor coach – or charabanc as it was originally known – there has been no shortage of tour companies which have included John O' Groats on their itinerary. Clients are naturally curious to know what the top corner of Scotland looks like and many operators feature a drive along our far north coast in their programme. The first documented evidence of an extended motorcoach tour which visited John O' Groats Hotel dates from 1920 when this group of Falkirk area businessmen and their wives made what was then a major journey in this charabanc. It was owned (and driven) by Walter Alexander of Camelon, Falkirk – a name which was later to become extremely well-known in transport circles throughout the world. This particular vehicle, MS 1723, was Alexander's first new Leyland – one of many hundreds which were to follow in the famous 'Bluebird' fleet over the years.

Some of Scotland's most wonderful sandy coves and beaches are to be found on its far north coast. This view between Tongue and Durness looking west over the Atlantic Ocean near Rispond at the mouth of Loch Eriboll dates from the late 1920s when the road surface of what is now the A838 was rough and stony, as may be seen. However that was no deterrent to the occupants of YH 2851, a London-registered 1928 Daimler 20 h.p. tourer with hood down to enjoy the sunshine. It would hardly be recommended to park on a bend at such a location today, but even now one of the attractions of this route 'along the top' is its relative freedom from traffic.

The phrase 'off the beaten track' may be applied to the minor single-track road leading north-west from Brora along the north side of Loch Brora via Gordonbush to Balnacoil and then south to Rogart in Strath Fleet. This scene from 1953 shows the former suspension bridge which was situated where the Black Water joins the River Brora at Balnacoil. It was for pedestrian use only, and vehicle traffic had to negotiate the adjacent Balnacoil Ford. In this scene a Ford Prefect of the early 1950s (the same car is seen in the picture opposite) is cautiously progressing through the waters. A new bridge for all traffic was opened at this location in May 1970, obviating the use of the ford.

Scotland's Atlantic coastline is so deeply indented by sea lochs that the ferries which operate there have historically been important links on journeys which would take much longer if the road were followed around the head of the intervening loch. Over the years some of those ferries have been replaced by bridges and of course this now even applies to the Lochalsh crossing to the Isle of Skye. Another example of a bridge link is at Kylesku in Sutherland where the former ferry was replaced in 1984. This view from the north landing in 1955 looks across to the Kylesku Hotel side and shows the *Maid of Kylesku* which plied back and forth across the waters at the head of Loch Cairnbawn, where it meets Lochs Glendhu and Glencoul. Thanks to the efforts of the Royal Scottish Automobile Club the first car ferry (built in 1923 by Dickie Bros. of Tarbert, Loch Fyne) was introduced at this crossing in 1924. In the 1930s it passed to the control of Sutherland County Council and was for some time the only free ferry in Scotland, with motorists and their vehicles enjoying this privilege until 1975. The vessel continued to operate until July 1984 when Kylesku Bridge opened with the inevitable withdrawal of the ferry service. The car waiting on the jetty is CTS 827, a Ford Prefect of 1953, and although today's modern bridge speeds the journey between Inchnadamph and Scourie, those with time to spare would no doubt agree that the old ferries had an undeniable aura of their own with of course a human touch impossible to enjoy when crossing concrete.

The Highland Railway was formed in June 1865 by the amalgamation of the Inverness & Aberdeen Junction Railway and the Inverness & Perth Junction Railway. The through service from Inverness to Wick and Thurso started in July 1874. About to leave Wick station in Edwardian days is HR 124 named *Loch Laggan*, resplendent in its pea-green livery with black bands and red and white lining. It was one of fifteen large 4-4-0 engines which were the last to be designed by locomotive superintendent David Jones, who served from 1870 until 1896. They were built by Dübs of Glasgow in 1896 and at the time were the company's most powerful locos. The Highland Railway, whose route mileage was just over 500, was included in the London, Midland & Scottish Railway after the formation of the four large railway groups in 1923.

This 0-4-4 saddle tank engine was built for the Highland Railway at Inverness in 1890. Defying superstition, it was numbered 13 and appropriately named *Strathpeffer*, as it served on that branch line from Dingwall. In 1901 it was rebuilt at Inverness and in 1903 was renumbered 53 and renamed *Lybster* when sent to work the Wick & Lybster Light Railway, where it remained until the railway grouping of 1923. This branch line of 13 miles and 63 chains opened in July 1903 and served the intermediate fishing and crofting communities of Thrumster, Ulbster, Mid Clyth and Occumster en route. It carried reasonable loadings until competition arrived in the mid-1920s in the form of motorbuses owned by Josiah Robertson of Wick and James Begg of Port Dunbar, which siphoned away much of the rail passenger traffic. Nevertheless the service survived on the branch until April 1944. This scene shows the arrival at Lybster station of the first train from Wick on 1 July 1903.

At one time there were no less than 40 intermediate stations and platforms on the main railway line between Inverness, Wick and Thurso, but this number has dropped considerably over the years. One of the stations which no longer exists is the Mound, between Rogart and Golspie. Situated at the head of Loch Fleet, the Mound takes its name from the 1,000 yard long road – and later also rail – embankment built by Thomas Telford in 1815 to obviate the use of the 'Little Ferry'. Passengers for Skelbo, Embo and Dornoch would transfer from their main line trains at the Mound and travel on the light railway to their destination. Opened in June 1902, this 7¾ mile branch line existed until June 1960 and was worked for many years by Highland Railway 0-4-4 tank locomotives, although two former Great Western Railway 0-6-0 pannier tanks (1646 and 1649) took over during the final years of operation. 1649 is seen at the Mound in August 1959 with the 2.05 p.m. to Dornoch connecting with the northbound 10.40 a.m. Inverness to Wick and Thurso.

Although the former Highland Railway – largely encouraged by the construction enterprises of the 3rd Duke of Sutherland – had linked Inverness with Thurso and Wick as early as 1874, no extensive system of road passenger transport existed until Inverness & District Motor Services Ltd. was formed in 1925. Initially operating between Inverness and Dingwall, the company did not reach north into Sutherland until 1929, when an extension was made from Tain to Dornoch. This new service represented a considerable saving in time compared to the railway route, which heads inland from Ardgay to Lairg and then doubles back towards the coast at the Mound. This scene shows one of the first I&D buses to operate the new extension to Dornoch in 1929 as it passes the Bridge Hotel in Bonar Bridge. It was ST 5313, one of three similar Albion PM 28 type vehicles then in the fleet which was painted in a smart livery described as 'two shades of scarlet with cream window-surrounds and white roof'. That same year the London, Midland & Scottish Railway acquired a 50% shareholding in the bus company and in April 1930 the 18-strong fleet of Inverness & District constituted the basis of the newly-formed Highland Transport Co. Ltd., which immediately set out to establish new services in the northern counties.

Somewhat surprisingly, Wick town council did not purchase their first motorised fire engine until as late as 1934. It was PG 4285, a second-hand appliance with a 40 gallon tank built by Dennis of Guildford and first registered in Surrey in 1929. Apparently the cost was £400 and at the same time the council bought 600 feet of 2½" hose for £54 and six waterproof coats for £12! Messrs R. S. Waters were successful with their tender to erect a fire engine shed on the opposite side of the River Wick from Martha Terrace, also for £12. In this view we see the Dennis at the Riverside in Wick giving demonstrations to the townsfolk shortly after its arrival in 1934, with firemaster John Bain and assistant firemaster David Bruce in charge. Further demonstrations elsewhere in the county were given over the next few days at locations including Watten, Halkirk, Thurso, Castletown (where according to the *John O' Groat Journal* 'the whole population of the village turned out'), John O' Groats, Berriedale and Lybster.

Although photographed in Wick at the war memorial, this happy group (even the horses seem to be smiling) was returning on the long journey home to Aberdeenshire after a country show at an unknown northern location in the late 1930s. The lorry carrying the Clydesdales has a demountable cattle float body fitted to its flat platform for the occasion. RG 3903 was owned by Wm. Wisely & Sons Ltd., a well-known haulier from Aberdeen and was a 1933 Leyland Beaver. Wisely had originally started his haulage business with horse-drawn lorries, later progressing to motor vehicles. Working as a general haulage and timber contractor, much business was done to and from Aberdeen docks. His vehicles carried a pale green livery.

The year is 1929. A busy period is captured by the camera in Wick High Street prior to the departure of the various country buses which are loading up both passengers and goods for the outlying villages. The roofs of William Johnstone's Chevrolet SK 1468, and Andrew Dunnet's similar Chevrolet SK 1231 behind, are both laden with boxes and tea chests. Johnstone's bus ran to Thurso via Kirk, Bower and Castletown, while Dunnet served Reiss and Keiss. SK 1467 on the left is a Bean (built in the late 1920s and early 30s in Dudley, Staffordshire), owned by Walter Wares, Castletown, who ran there via Watten, Bower and Thurso, while just visible in the Market Place outside Greenlees 'Easiephit' shoe shop is Donald Allan's bus from Gillock which served Wick and Thurso via Sibster, Gersta and Bower. In 1933 all of these owners, with the exception of Dunnet, sold their small businesses to the predatory Highland Transport Co. of Inverness which was expanding its territory in the north.

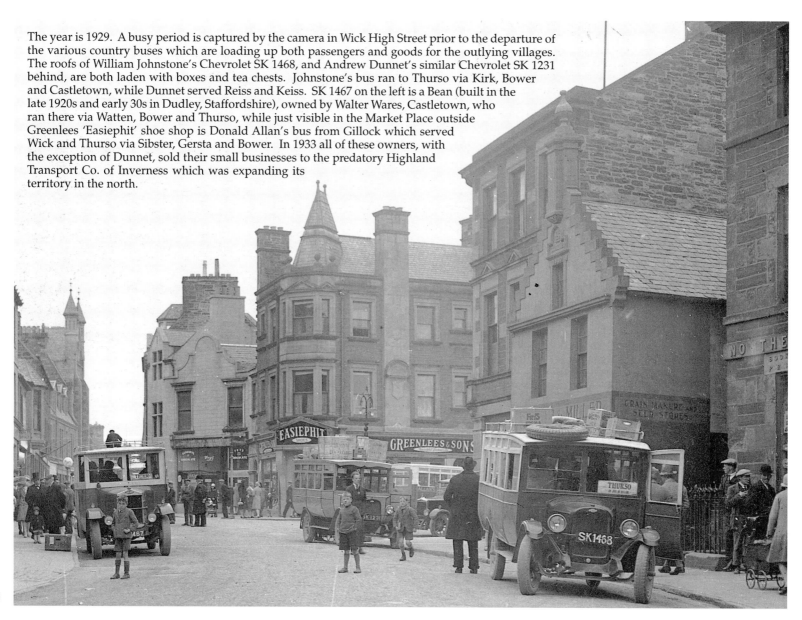

During the dark days of World War II, between 1939 and 1945, motor vehicles had to comply with extra regulations and restrictions which included white-edged mudguards and masked headlamps. In addition, the Highland Transport bus fleet lost its attractive red and cream colour scheme for an austerity grey livery. These temporary changes may be seen in this view of Highland Transport Albion no. 9 at John O' Groats about to depart on the 4.35 p.m. journey to Thurso on 29 June 1944 (despite showing 'Castletown' as the destination). Male and female forces personnel may be seen boarding, no doubt travelling to the wartime RAF base at Castletown. Wartime photographs are relatively rare since film was both expensive and scarce, but this scene was taken at the northern end of an epic journey made by a veteran transport enthusiast and friend of mine, John Gillham of London. He travelled by local public service buses (99 in total!) all the way from his home in the capital to John O' Groats and Thurso and back again during blackout conditions. Fortunately he fully recorded his journey and on checking his notes found that he paid the Highland Transport conductress 1/6 d for the fare from John O' Groats to Thurso. He has kept the ticket ever since! ST 6892 was one of two Albion Valkyrie models which had been new to the Highland Transport Company in 1932 (see overleaf), both with bodywork by Cowieson of Glasgow. Later, Highland Transport completely rebuilt no. 9 in their

Needlefields workshop, Inverness, and changed its rear entrance to the front, as seen here. Its reliability and long life ensured that it was taken into the Highland Omnibuses fleet on the formation of that company in 1952.

Highland Transport operations in Caithness were widened after several small operators in the county sold their businesses to the company in the early 1930s. The first to sell was Hunter & Knox of Wick who ran under the fleetname 'Pioneer'. This firm had come north from Fife and attempted regular services on several routes including Wick–Halkirk–Thurso; Wick–Kirk–Bower–Castletown–Thurso; and Bettyhill–Melvich–Thurso. The mixed fleet included second-hand Reo, Chevrolet, Beardmore and Albion buses, none of which was sound enough to be acquired when Highland Transport took over in 1930. This scene in Station Square, Brora, was taken specially to mark the journey of the first four buses en route north from their base in Inverness to Caithness in 1930 to work Highland's initial services in the county, between Wick and Thurso. They were Albion model 26 types and their Highland numbers were, left to right, 39, 40, 46, 41 (ST 5645, 5674, 6102, 5751).

Bridge Street, Wick photographed in 1937 with decorations commemorating the Coronation of King George VI. Outside the town hall is ST 6983, Highland Transport Albion Valkyrie no. 10, which was new in 1932 and was later to become a breakdown lorry with the company after withdrawal from passenger service. The cars are APK 728, a Riley of 1933 from Surrey and locally-registered SK 2028, a 1935 Austin.

The Highland Transport Company and the state-owned Highland Omnibuses Ltd. which followed from 1952 were both keen operators of double and single-deck buses built by Guy Motors of Wolverhampton. This 1962 view at the same location in Bridge Street, Wick, taken 25 years after the one opposite, shows Highland Omnibuses E68 leaving the town hall bus stop for the terminus at the railway station having worked its way from Thurso via Castletown. ASD 405 was a wartime Guy Arab which had been new in 1943 to Western SMT of Kilmarnock, receiving new bodywork in 1951 by Eastern Coach Works of Lowestoft. In 1960 it was sold to Highland Omnibuses where it remained until finally withdrawn in 1965.

Highland Transport opened up the main road service on the A9 between Inverness, Wick and Thurso in stages until in 1933 the final gap (between Brora and Helmsdale) was linked. At that time the Inverness–Thurso journey was timetabled at a lengthy 9½ hours! This of course was long before the bridging of the Firths and was no competition for the train, unlike today's Citylink service which takes only 3½ hours and is consequently speedier than Scotrail. In 1952 Highland Transport was reconstituted as Highland Omnibuses Ltd., the newly-formed member of the nationalised Scottish Bus Group. Seen when new in 1957 at Spinningdale running south to Inverness from Dornoch is LST 503 (B9), one of six similar Park Royal bodied AEC Reliances in the HOL fleet.

The far northern counties of Caithness and Sutherland are no strangers to heavy winter snowfalls and the problems these bring. Seen in the late 1950s on the snowbound main A882 Wick to Thurso road between Bilbster and Watten is a group of Highland Omnibuses drivers with their temporarily abandoned vehicles (on Dounreay contract services) waiting for the passing snowplough to clear the way ahead. The leading bus is one of several 1949 Commer Commandos with Scottish Aviation bodies which had passed to HOL from Alexander of Falkirk. The Caithness County Council snow plough of the late 1940s was one of a large fleet of former US Army left-hand drive Mack trucks owned by the Scottish Home Department and allocated to various councils throughout the country.

SK 2433 was originally a Fordson BB type bus with only seven seats plus a mail compartment which was delivered to Wm. Wilson of the Station Hotel, Thurso in 1938. It passed to the Highland Transport Co. when it acquired Wilson's bus service in 1940. Although numbered as bus no. 95 with Highland, it was not operated as such, but converted to a small lorry, as seen here at Thurso railway station (the most northerly in Britain) where it would meet the trains to collect and deliver goods. It remained in the fleet until transferred to Highland Omnibuses in 1952 and lasted nearly three more years under their ownership.

The newly-formed Highland Transport Company arrived in Caithness in 1930 and one year later built a depot in Janet Street at Lovers Lane, Thurso for their expanding services in the county. Today, Rapson's Highland Country Bus depot is still located on that original site, although it is now considerably larger. This view shows the interior of the garage in 1961 when Highland Omnibuses Ltd. owned the premises, and the buses visible are a good representation of HOL vehicles at that period. The fleet had been steadily expanding through the 1950s, partly because of the construction and growth of the United Kingdom Atomic Energy Authority site at Dounreay at a time when fewer folk owned cars, accordingly placing a greater demand on public transport. Seen here are three Alexander bodied AEC Reliances, three Northern Counties bodied wartime Guy Arab double deckers, a Park Royal bodied AEC Reliance, a Duple bodied AEC Regal, a Strachan bodied Guy and a Churchill bodied Austin. This last vehicle was originally in the fleet of MacRae & Dick, Inverness, which along with Highland Transport was one of the joint constituents which in 1952 formed Highland Omnibuses Ltd., youngest member of the nationalised Scottish Bus Group.

The name Dunnet of Keiss was familiar from the 1920s onwards, providing motorised passenger transport between the Caithness crab village and the town of Wick. In 1942 the service was extended to and from John O' Groats after John Smith Banks of Groats gave up his run from there to Wick. However, Dunnet's history goes back to Victorian times since in the 1880s the family commenced a general goods carrying service mainly between Wick railway station and Keiss village. Here we see Charles Dunnet heading homewards in early Edwardian days with his pair of horses drawing a cart laden with a variety of items.

SK 1905 was a Thornycroft Manly which Dunnet purchased as a new chassis in 1933, but which was fitted with a second-hand body from a previous 'Thorny' in the fleet. Jamesie Mowat of Keiss, who drove for many years with Dunnet, poses proudly alongside when the bus was new.

Scenes like this were not uncommon in bad weather before the new bridge was opened over the River Wester (which flows east from Loch Wester to the North Sea) between Keiss and Reiss. Here we see the now bypassed old Brig O' Wester in the background as Dunnet's AEC Regal driven by Willie Grant of Keiss ploughs through the flooded section on its journey from John O' Groats to Wick in the late 1950s. The bus was DUP 137, one of two identical AECs (the other being DUP 130) which joined Dunnet's fleet from the Northern General Transport Co. of Gateshead, Co. Durham, where they had been new in 1939. Replacement bodywork was fitted in 1949 by Pickering of Wishaw and when sold in 1957 they made the journey north to Keiss, where they gave good service for a further few years. Back in the 1920s another Keiss operator was Donald (Dane) Finlayson who ran to Wick with model T Fords, one of which was known to the local schoolboys as 'Kentucky'.

Two buses in the once-familiar fleet of Dunnet of Keiss. Seen here in the mid-1950s at the garage and fuel pumps in Keiss village is the first double decker to have operated in their fleet. This was GNU 452, a Metro-Cammell bodied AEC Regent which had been new in 1939 to Chesterfield Corporation, passing to A. & C. McLennan of Spitalfield in 1952 and then to Dunnet's until withdrawn in 1957. The single decker was SK 2886, one of two wartime utility bodied Bedford OWBs delivered new to Dunnet's. The firm saw a brief period of expansion after deregulation of the bus industry in 1986, but sadly their light blue and cream buses ceased operating in 1999 ending a span of over a century's involvement with commercial transport in Caithness. Today Rapson's Highland Country Buses operate the routes formerly served by Dunnet's.

Three of the once-familiar and much-missed red and cream Sutherland Transport & Trading Co. buses sit in the summer sunshine outside Lairg post office in the mid-1950s. Foremost is NS 1931, a Bedford OWB dating from 1944. Similar model NS 1910 sits alongside, with the doors to its mail and luggage compartment open for loading. Both these buses had wartime utility bodywork built by SMT of Edinburgh while DRS 843 behind was a 1950 Leyland Comet bodied by Plaxton of Scarborough. Amongst the wide variety of goods carried daily on the ST&T bus network to and from Bettyhill, Durness, Kinlochbervie, Lochinver, Tongue and Scourie were perishables such as salmon for the southbound train, and milk for all the country destinations. Laundry to and from the various sporting hotels was also a major load, whilst of course Her Majesty's Mails were most important of all. In the early days, when the services were operated by Albion wagonettes similar to that on p13, it was apparently common practice for the drivers never to leave Lairg for the outlying areas without the reassurance of a traditional hip flask. This was perhaps understandable as they were completely open to the elements, and snowbound winter journeys must have been particularly arduous.

Not a nasty accident as many may imagine, but the one-time daily routine at Lairg railway station when Sutherland Transport buses would reverse across the lines to load and unload directly at the platform the wide variety of goods and parcels carried to and from the various country destinations. This early 1960s view shows NS 2388 on the left (one of two identical Albion Victors bodied by Croft of Glasgow) recently arrived on the local service from Lairg post office, while on the tracks is Duple bodied Bedford NS 4745 from Lochinver. The ST&T buses connected with the arriving mail trains on the Wick to Inverness service, due to arrive at Lairg 11.57 southbound and 12.57 northbound at that period.

Time to talk. A scene from more leisurely days as the Sutherland Transport bus en route from Lairg to Scourie pauses at Merkland in the summer of 1935. Driver Alex Mackay of Scourie leans against his cab while the kilted Colonel Cuthbert of the former Badcall Manse (now the Eddrachillis Hotel) chats to Mrs Gartan (of the HP sauce family and owners of Merkland Estate). The bus was NS 1282, an Albion of 1931 with bodywork built by Cadogan of Perth.

In addition to the bus fleet, the Sutherland Transport & Trading Co. also operated lorries from its base in Lairg, where the depot building was a former aircraft hangar. The lorry fleet was mainly engaged in fish traffic from Kinlochbervie to Hull and Grimsby and in timber haulage. When the Duke of Westminster's Estates acquired the business in 1951 some lorries came north to Sutherland from one of the Duke's English businesses, Pulford Estates Ltd. At the same time, more lorries joined the ST&T Co. with the acquisition of a local fleet (mainly Austins) owned by J. MacLeod. NS 5006, seen at Lairg, was an ERF 8-wheeler with LAD cab new in 1962 and powered by a Gardner 150 engine. Note the old phone numbers on the cab door – Lairg 65 and 66. The ST&T lorry fleet was painted in a dark green livery, as opposed to the cream and red of their buses. Other commercials in the fleet included AEC, Albion, Bedford and Leyland vehicles.

One of the earlier Sutherland Transport lorries was SK 1763, an Albion which had started life in 1931 as a 20-seat bus with mail compartment operated by J. J. Robertson of Wick on his mail and passenger service to Helmsdale. After Robertson sold out to the Highland Transport Company in 1932, it continued in use as a bus until 1940 when it was rebuilt and converted to a lorry in their Needlefields workshops, Inverness, before purchase by the Sutherland Transport & Trading Co. It ran for them throughout the war years (note the necessary masked headlamps for wartime driving) until sold in 1946 to an Inverness timber haulier. This scene shows it at Needlefields displaying Sutherland trade plates 002 NS prior to delivery to Lairg for the ST&T Co.

The grandly named 'North Coast Road Motor Service' was operated by D. R. Simpson of Wick to Keiss, John O' Groats, Canisbay, Mey, Dunnet and Castletown. Simpson was a well-known local businessman with a variety of other interests which included fishing boats, fish curing, salmon fisheries and ironmongers. He was part-owner of Scotland's first steam herring drifter, the *Content* of 1899. Simpson's bus operation was a relatively short-lived enterprise and the service passed in 1931 to his former driver Peter Gunn of Castletown and then in 1936 to George Begg of Rattar. Seen here is SK 1207, a model T Ford 13-seater which had been new to Simpson in 1926. Entry and exit was by a centre door at the very back, while two rows of five seats faced each other on either side of the bus, with room for another three beside the driver. A rail around the roof outside allowed passengers to carry all sorts of items above, as may be seen. The model T chassis was popular with several bus operators in the county at that time, including Alex Robertson of Wick, George Dower of Halkirk, Andrew Dunnet of Keiss and R. S. Waters of Wick to name but a few.

Dennis Morrison of Castletown stands at the door of SK 3073, his 1947 Duple bodied Bedford OB which plied the service from Thurso to Wick via Castletown, Lyth and Barrock. Campbell of Keiss had originally operated this route in the 1920s and it later passed to Donald Smith of Castletown before being continued by Donald Banks Morrison. Morrison's business is also now only a memory since Rapson's Highland Country Buses acquired the family firm in 2000.

A. R. McLeod & Sons of Helmsdale used this dark blue and white normal control (bonneted) Leyland Comet with Plaxton coachwork on schools services and also the passenger route in the 1960s between Helmsdale, Kildonan and Kinbrace where a connection was made with Dugald O'Brien's bus service – to Bettyhll via Strathnaver. AYJ 867 originally operated with Dickson's tours of Dundee to whom it was new in 1950; this photograph was taken in 1964 in McLeod's Helmsdale garage. McLeod's ceased trading in 1998.

One of three Bedford coaches operated in the 1960s on school contracts and private hire work by Seaforth MacGregor of Craigroyston, Dornoch. Sunday church runs were also maintained from Dornoch to Rearquhar and Birichen and from Dornoch to Embo, Fourpenny and Skelbo. NS 3924 was a neat 29-seat Duple Vista bodied Bedford bought new in 1959 and seen in 1964 at the Victoria Jubilee Fountain in Brora, outside the Grand Hotel (now renamed the Braes Hotel). MacGregor, whose fleet colours were light blue and buff, sold his business to Highland Omnibuses in 1967.

Peter Burr of Tongue formerly operated a combined passenger and goods service from Tongue to Thurso via Skerray, Bettyhill, Melvich and Reay (pioneered by Wilson of the Station Hotel, Thurso in 1913). Schoolchildren board outside the old Thurso post office in Sinclair Street as MVD 268 prepares to depart on its afternoon journey to Tongue on a sunny September day in 1964 while conductor Davie Henderson of Skerray chats to a lady passenger. This 41-seat Duple-bodied Bedford in Burr's dark green and off-white livery had its seating capacity reduced to 28 in order to incorporate a large luggage compartment at the rear for mails and parcels. Burr also ran a retail grocery store in Tongue, along with the petrol pumps, and in addition operated several lorries which provided both a local network plus a trunk service to Glasgow. In 1966 Burr's service was acquired by Highland Omnibuses Ltd.

photo by Brian McGinley, East Kilbride

D. Steven & Son is very much a familiar name in road haulage, specialising mainly in the carriage of fish. Based in Wick since the 1920s, when the horse and cart still ruled, Steven's red liveried lorries are to be seen throughout both Britain and Europe and well-known was their slogan 'O'er the Ord'. Seen here heading south having negotiated the infamous Auchenkilns roundabout near Cumbernauld is V74 JSK, a Scania 144, bearing the personalised fleetname Highland Princess.